At Sylvan, we believe that writing is one of life's most important and enriching abilities, and we're glad you've chosen our resources to help your child build this critically important skill. We know that the time you spend with your child reinforcing lessons learned in school will contribute to his or her success in writing. Clear handwriting, in addition to enabling others to read one's work, helps develop a student's visual memory, which is vital for effective reading. A successful writer is able to communicate with others in meaningful ways—and will better experience the world of reading as well.

We use a research-based, step-by-step process in teaching handwriting at Sylvan that helps students become more confident in their handwriting skills. Our Sylvan workbooks are designed to help you work with your child to build the skills and confidence that will contribute to his or her success in school.

Included with your purchase of this workbook is a coupon for a discount at a participating Sylvan center. We hope you will use this coupon to further your child's academic journey. Let us partner with you to support the development of a confident, well-prepared writer.

The Sylvan Team

Kindergarten-1st Grade Success with Uppercase Letters

Published in the United States by Random House, Inc., New York, and in Canada by Random House of Canada Limited, Toronto.

www.tutoring.sylvanlearning.com

Created by Smarterville Productions LLC
Producer & Editorial Direction: The Linguistic Edge
Producer: TJ Trochlil McGreevy
Writer: Erin Lassiter
Cover and Interior Illustrations: Shawn Finley, Tim Goldman, and Duendes del Sur
Layout and Art Direction: SunDried Penguin

First Edition

ISBN: 978-0-307-47934-1
ISSN: 2156-6399

This book is available at special discounts for bulk purchases for sales promotions or premiums. For more information, write to Special Markets/Premium Sales, 1745 Broadway, MD 6-2, New York, New York 10019 or e-mail specialmarkets@randomhouse.com.

PRINTED IN CHINA

10 9 8 7 6 5 4 3 2 1

Contents

Write the Letter L

TRACE the uppercase letter **L**. Start at the green arrow labeled with a number 1.

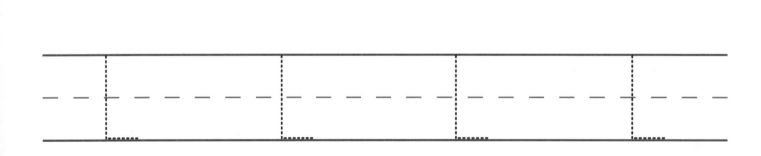

Now WRITE four uppercase **L**'s.

1   2   3   4

Letter Blocks

WRITE **L** in the empty blocks.

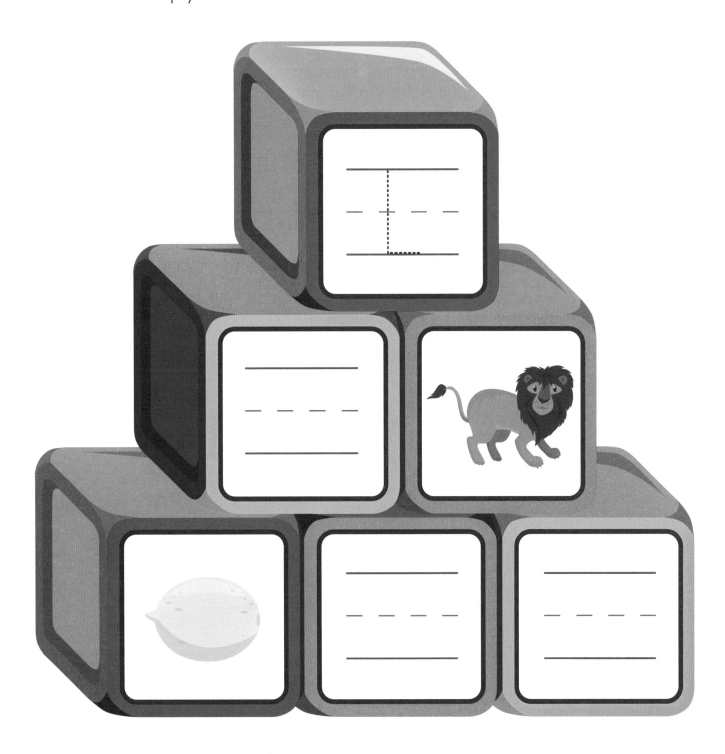

Uppercase L

Letter Connection

WRITE L in each space to connect the ladybugs.

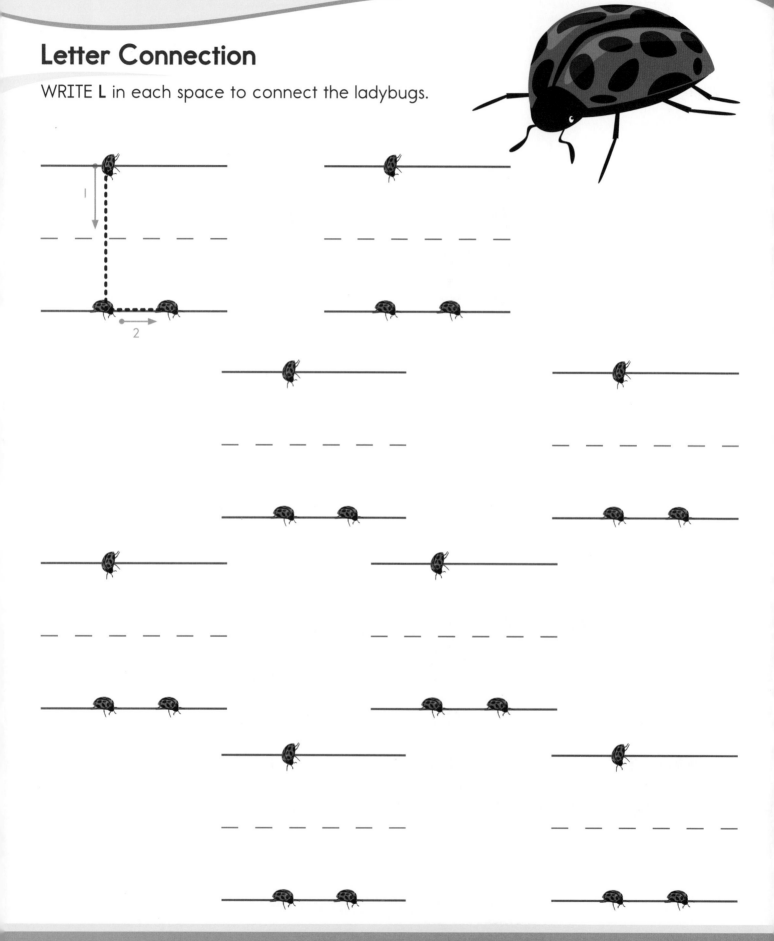

Tongue Twisting Time

WRITE **L** in each space to
complete the tongue twister.

‾Lucy ‾Lion

‾Likes ‾Learning

‾Letter

‾Lessons

Uppercase T

Write the Letter T

TRACE the uppercase letter T. Start at the green arrow labeled with a number 1.

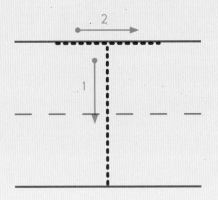

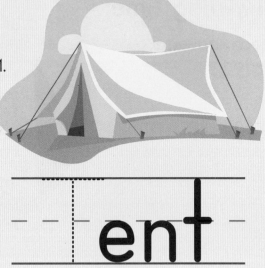

Tent

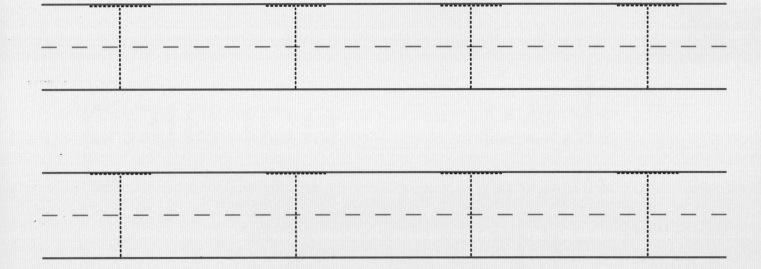

Now WRITE four uppercase T's.

1   2   3   4

6

Letter Blocks

WRITE **T** in the empty blocks.

Grocery List

WRITE **T** in each space to finish the grocery list.

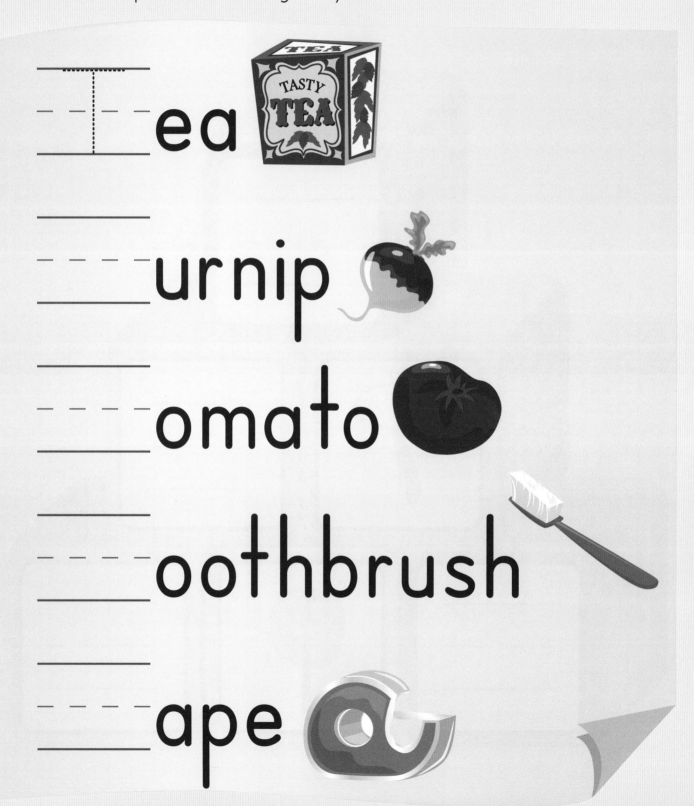

_____ea

_____urnip

_____omato

_____oothbrush

_____ape

T Is for Train

WRITE **T** on each train car.

Write the Letter I

TRACE the uppercase letter **I**. Start at the green arrow labeled with a number 1.

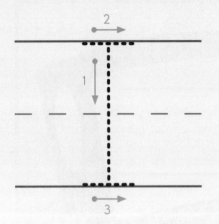

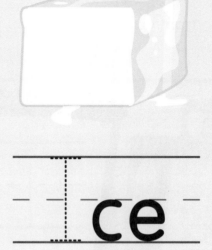

ce

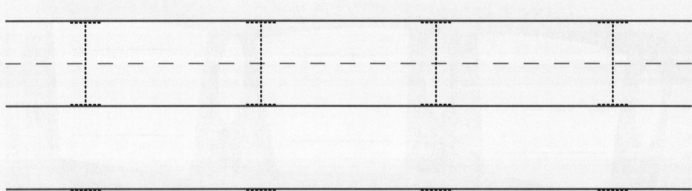

Now WRITE four uppercase **I**'s.

1   2   3   4

Letter Blocks

WRITE **I** in the empty blocks.

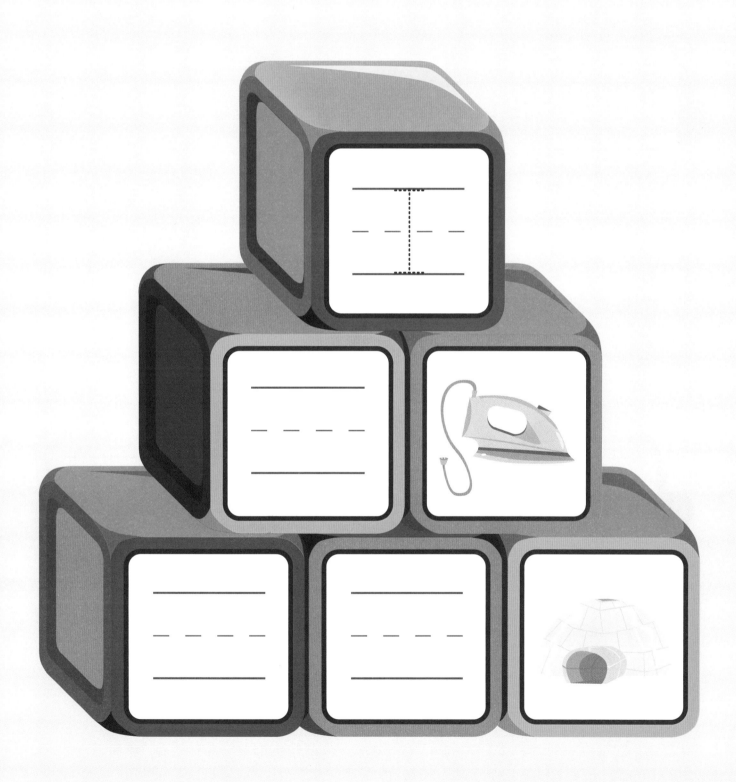

I Is for Ice Cream

WRITE **I** on each ice cream cone.

Name Game

WRITE **I** in each space to see each child's name.

HELLO

I an

HELLO

da

HELLO

rene

HELLO

ke

HELLO

saiah

HELLO

ngrid

Uppercase F

Write the Letter F

TRACE the uppercase letter **F**. Start at the green arrow labeled with a number 1.

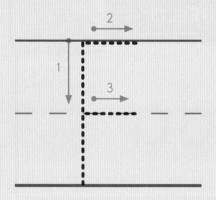

Fish

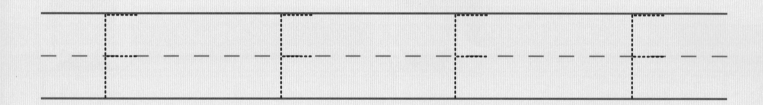

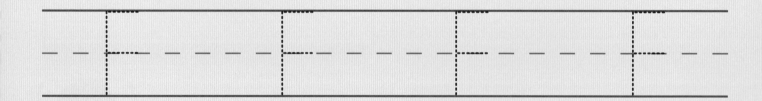

Now WRITE four uppercase **F**'s.

1	2	3	4

Letter Blocks

WRITE **F** in the empty blocks.

F Is for Fruit

WRITE **F** on each fruit bowl.

Write around the Wheel

WRITE **F** on each car on the Ferris wheel.

Write the Letter E

TRACE the uppercase letter **E**. Start at the green arrow labeled with a number 1.

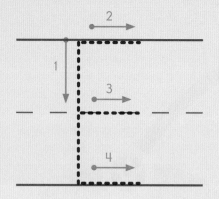

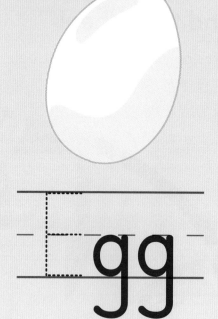

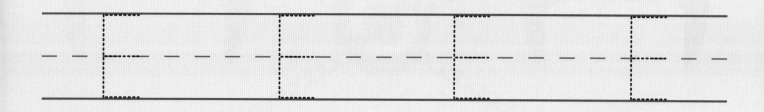

Now WRITE four uppercase **E**'s.

1	2	3	4

Letter Blocks

WRITE **E** in the empty blocks.

Uppercase E

Name Game

WRITE **E** in each space to see each child's name.

HELLO

Eva

HELLO

Eloise

HELLO

Eddie

HELLO

Evan

HELLO

Elias

HELLO

Emma

Deliver the Letter

WRITE **E** in each space to finish addressing the letter.

30¢

__Ellie __agle

123 __gg St.

__agleton, N__

68347

Uppercase H

Write the Letter H

TRACE the uppercase letter **H**. Start at the green arrow labeled with a number 1.

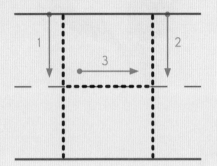

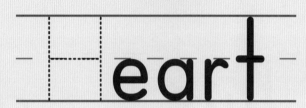

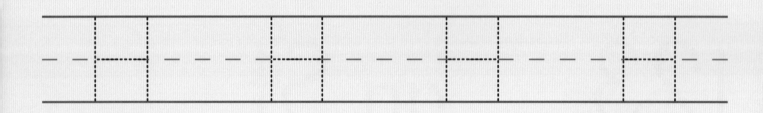

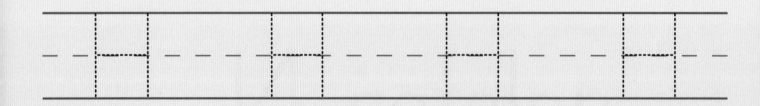

Now WRITE four uppercase **H**'s.

1   2   3   4

Letter Blocks

WRITE **H** in the empty blocks.

Uppercase H

Stitch It Up

WRITE **H** in each square to finish the quilt.

Tongue Twisting Time

WRITE **H** in each space to
complete the tongue twister.

Hilary

__en __elps

__arold __orse

__aul __ay

Skywriting

WRITE the letters in the clouds following each airplane.

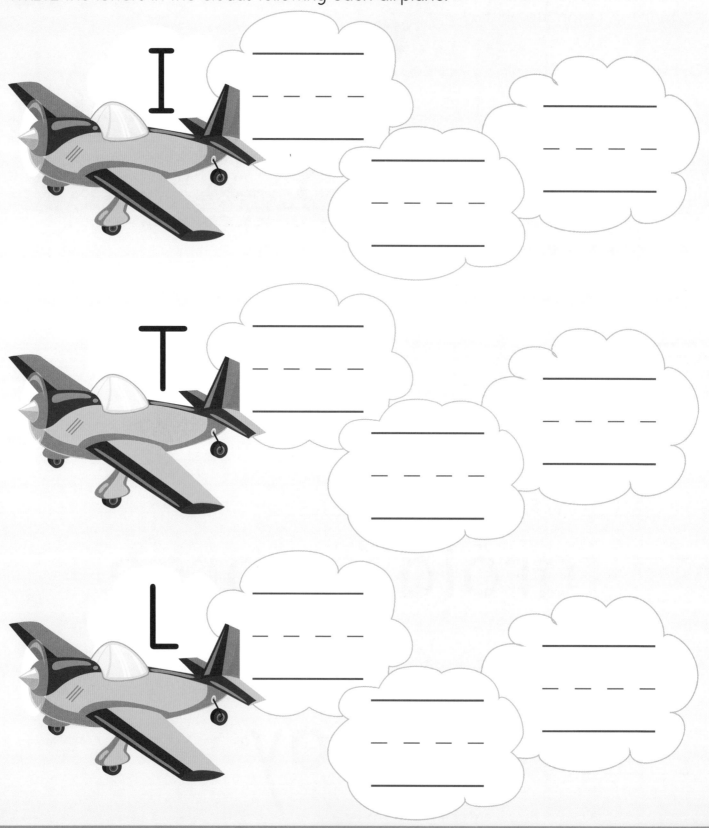

E

F

H

Write the Letter N

TRACE the uppercase letter **N**. Start at the green arrow labeled with a number 1.

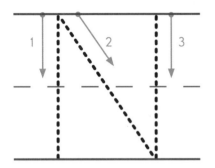

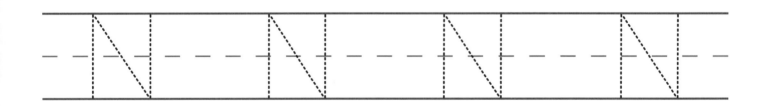

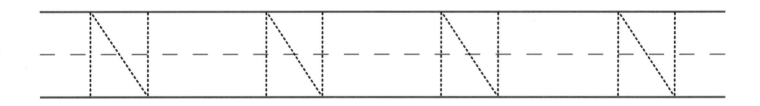

Now WRITE four uppercase **N**'s.

1   2   3   4

Letter Blocks

WRITE **N** in the empty blocks.

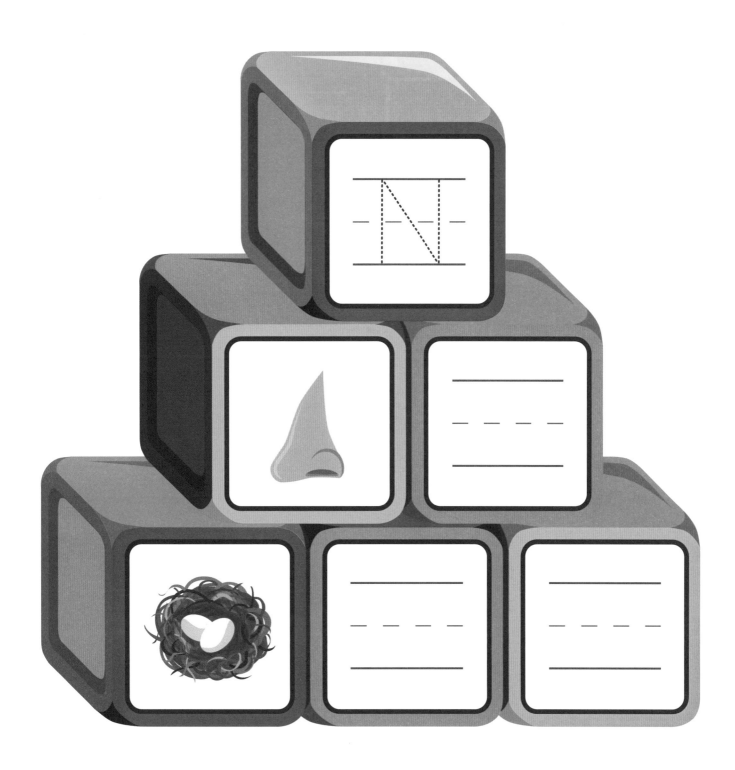

Uppercase N

Name Game

WRITE **N** in each space to see each child's name.

HELLO

Nate

HELLO

___adia

HELLO

___oah

HELLO

___eha

HELLO

___ikki

HELLO

___igel

Write around the Wheel

WRITE **N** on each car on the Ferris wheel.

Write the Letter M

TRACE the uppercase letter **M**. Start at the green arrow labeled with a number 1.

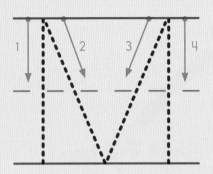

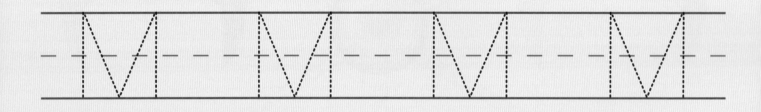

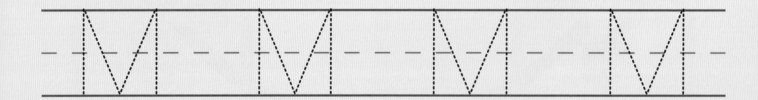

Now WRITE four uppercase **M**'s.

1   2   3   4

8

Letter Blocks

WRITE **M** in the empty blocks.

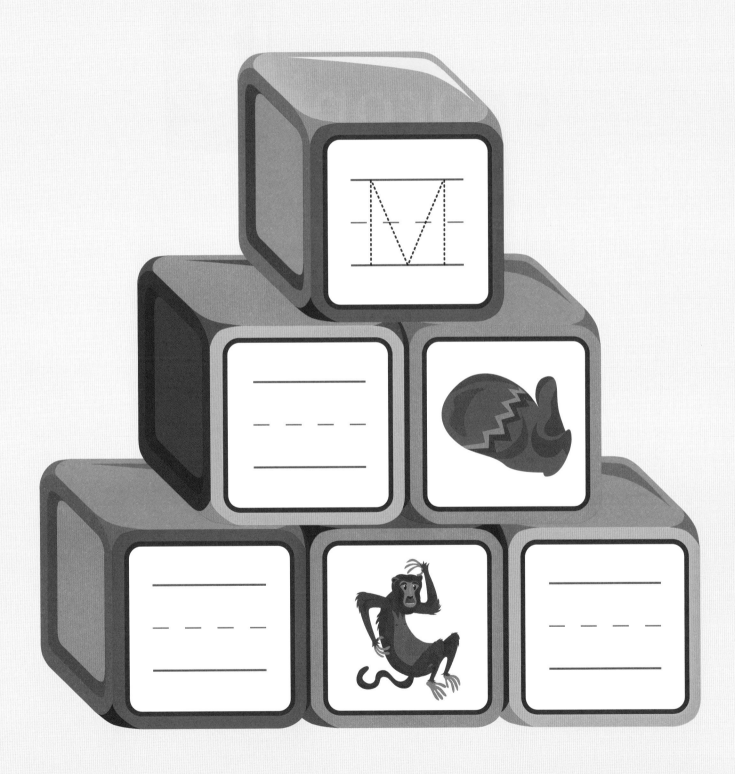

Uppercase M

Grocery List

WRITE **M** in each space to finish the grocery list.

M̶acaroni

____ ilk

____ uffin

____ ushrooms

____ ustard

Tongue Twisting Time

WRITE **M** in each space to
complete the tongue twister.

Marvin ___ole

___errily ___akes

___ud ___uffins

Write the Letter V

TRACE the uppercase letter **V**. Start at the green arrow labeled with a number 1.

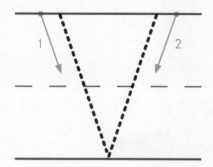

Vase

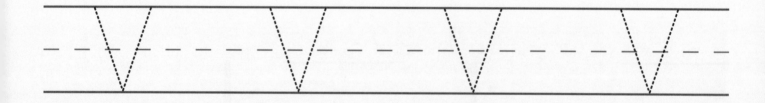

Now WRITE four uppercase **V**'s.

1   2   3   4

Letter Blocks

WRITE **V** in the empty blocks.

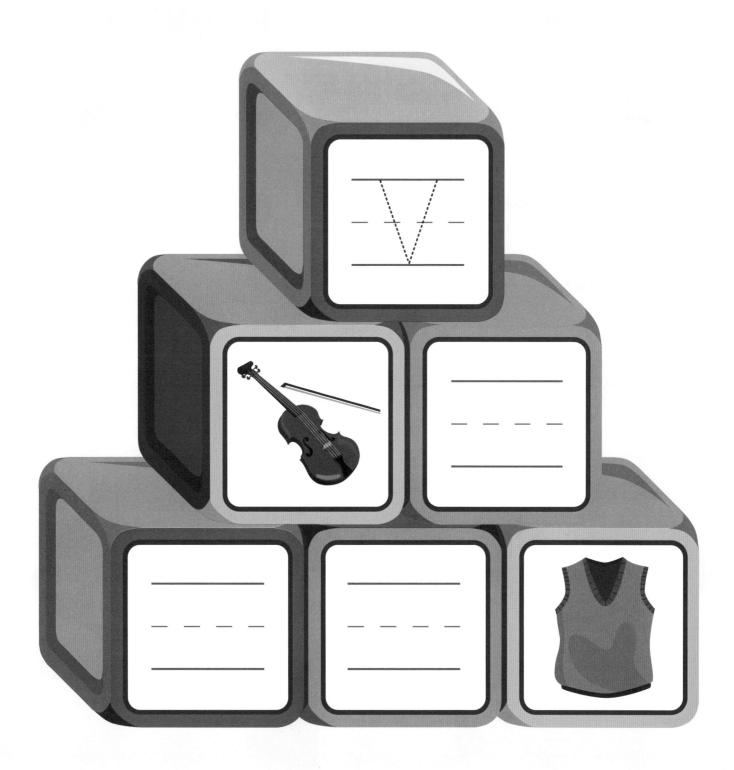

V Is for Volcano

WRITE **V** on each volcano.

Name Game

WRITE V in each space to see each child's name.

HELLO

__V__al

HELLO

___ernon

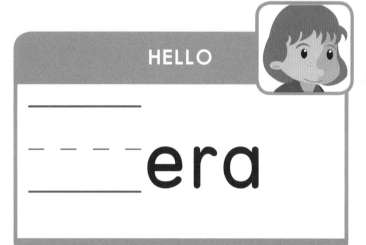

HELLO

___era

HELLO

___ictor

HELLO

___ivian

HELLO

___ita

Write the Letter W

TRACE the uppercase letter **W**. Start at the green arrow labeled with a number 1.

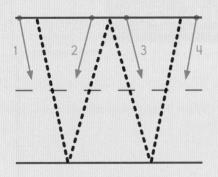

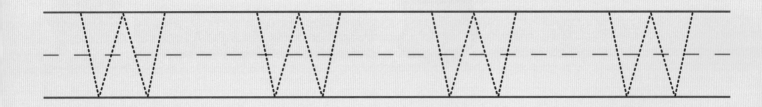

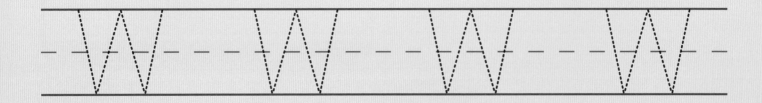

Now WRITE four uppercase **W**'s.

1   2   3   4

Letter Blocks

WRITE **W** in the empty blocks.

Deliver the Letter

WRITE W in each space to finish addressing the letter.

Wally __alrus

27 __ater __ay

__alla __alla, __A

99362

Tongue Twisting Time

WRITE **W** in each space to complete the tongue twister.

Wes __orm

__altzes __ith

__endy __asp

Write the Letter X

TRACE the uppercase letter **X**. Start at the green arrow labeled with a number 1.

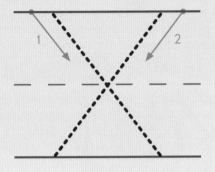

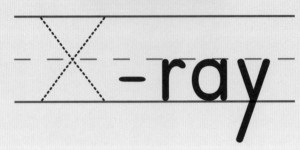
X-ray

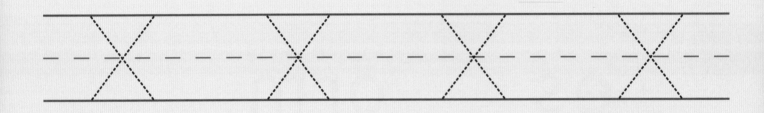

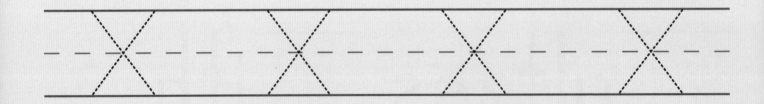

Now WRITE four uppercase **X**'s.

1   2   3   4

Letter Blocks

WRITE **X** in the empty blocks.

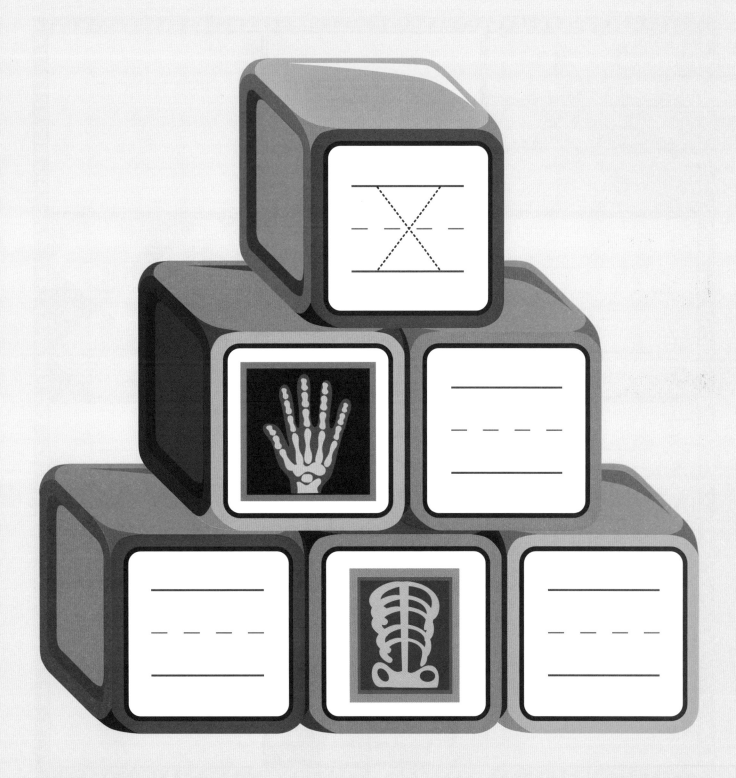

Uppercase X

Stitch It Up

WRITE **X** in each square to finish the quilt.

X on the Box

WRITE **X** on the side of each box.

Triple Play

TRACE each letter. Then WRITE it three times.

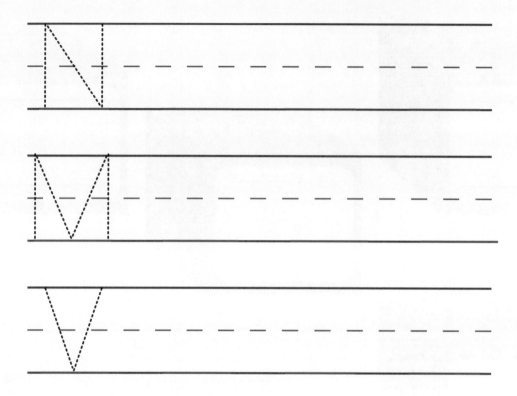

WRITE **N**, **M**, and **V** in the blocks.

Double Play

TRACE each letter. Then WRITE it three times.

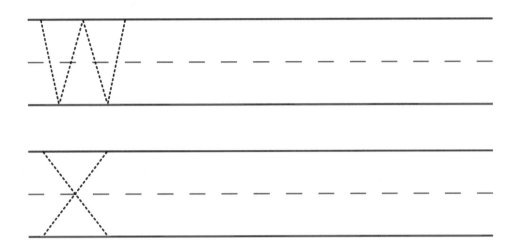

WRITE **W** and **X** in the blocks.

Uppercase Z

Write the Letter Z

TRACE the uppercase letter **Z**. Start at the green arrow labeled with a number 1.

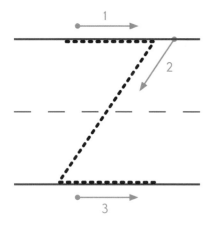

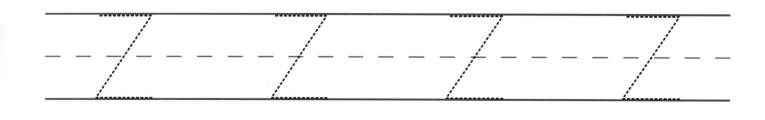

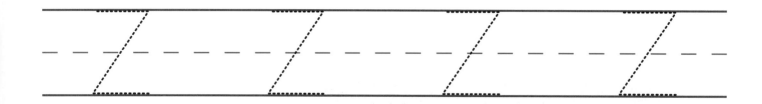

Now WRITE four uppercase **Z**'s.

1   2   3   4

Letter Blocks

WRITE **Z** in the empty blocks.

Uppercase Z

Stitch It Up

WRITE **Z** in each square to finish the quilt.

Name Game

WRITE **Z** in each space to see each child's name.

HELLO

Zach

HELLO

___elda

HELLO
___ane

HELLO

___afina

HELLO
___oey

HELLO

___eke

Write the Letter Y

TRACE the uppercase letter **Y**. Start at the green arrow labeled with a number 1.

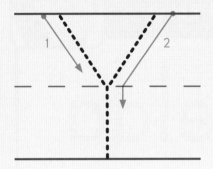

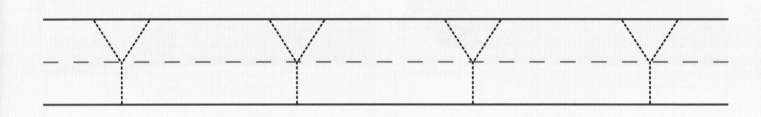

Now WRITE four uppercase **Y**'s.

1   2   3   4

Letter Blocks

WRITE Y in the empty blocks.

Y Is for Yo-yo

WRITE Y on each yo-yo.

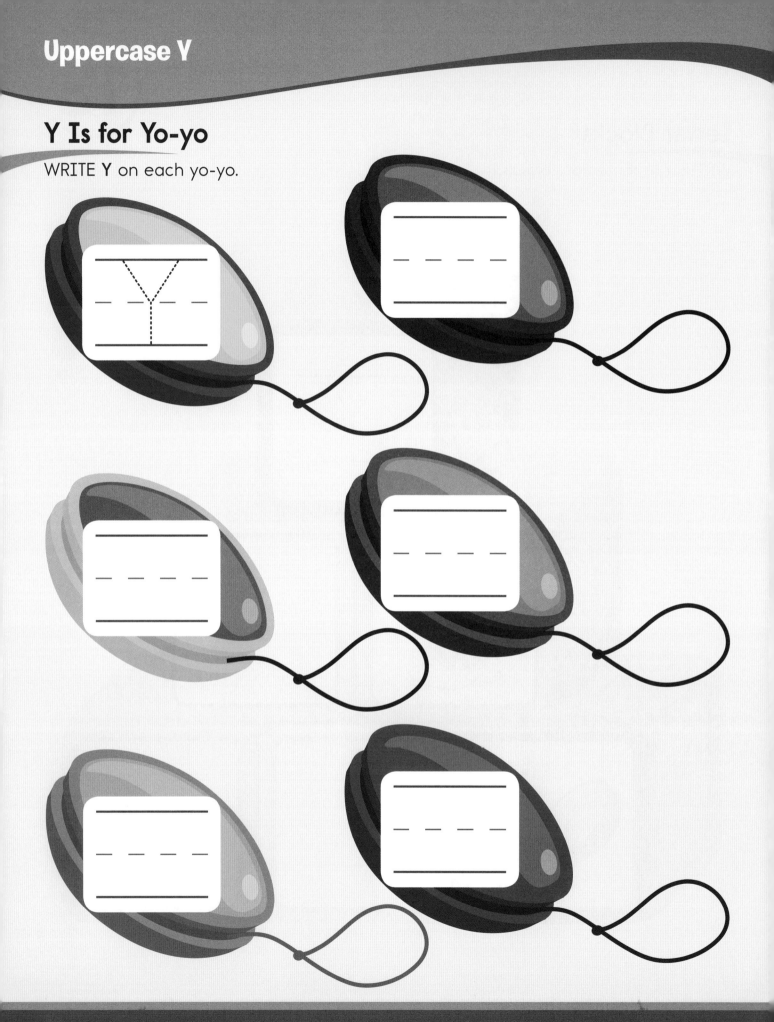

Tongue Twisting Time

WRITE Y in each space to complete the tongue twister.

Yetty

__ak __earns

for __ummy

__ellow __ams

Write the Letter A

TRACE the uppercase letter **A**. Start at the green arrow labeled with a number 1.

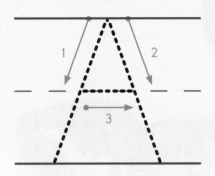

Apple

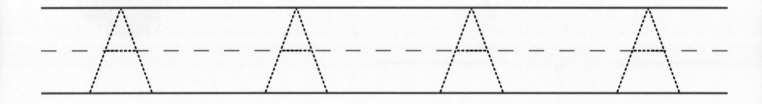

Now WRITE four uppercase **A**'s.

1   2   3   4

Letter Blocks

WRITE **A** in the empty blocks.

Deliver the Letter

WRITE A in each space to finish addressing the letter.

__Archie __nt

4l6 __pple __ve.

__nthill, __Z

85086

A Is for Anthill

WRITE **A** on each anthill.

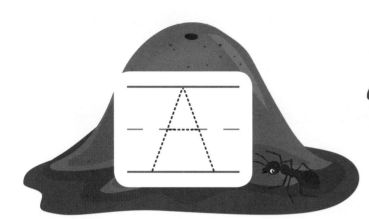

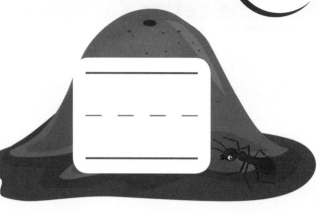

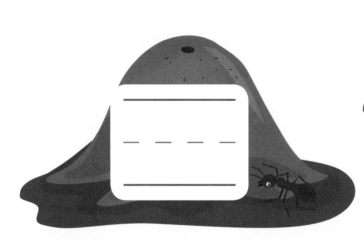

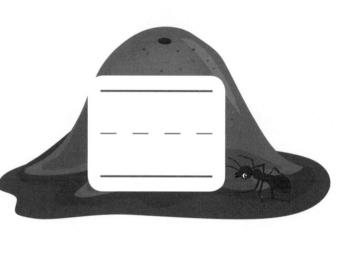

Uppercase K

Write the Letter K

TRACE the uppercase letter K. Start at the green arrow labeled with a number 1.

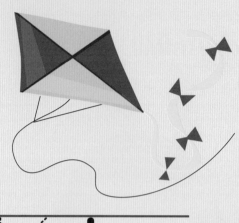

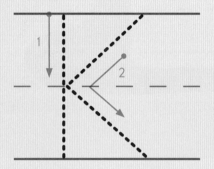

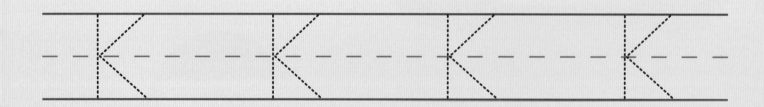

Now WRITE four uppercase K's.

1   2   3   4

62

Letter Blocks

WRITE **K** in the empty blocks.

Uppercase K

Name Game

WRITE **K** in each space to see each child's name.

HELLO

Kayla

HELLO

___elly

HELLO

___enji

HELLO

___urt

HELLO

___eisha

HELLO

___en

K Is for Kangaroo

WRITE **K** on each kangaroo.

Skywriting

WRITE the letters in the clouds following each airplane.

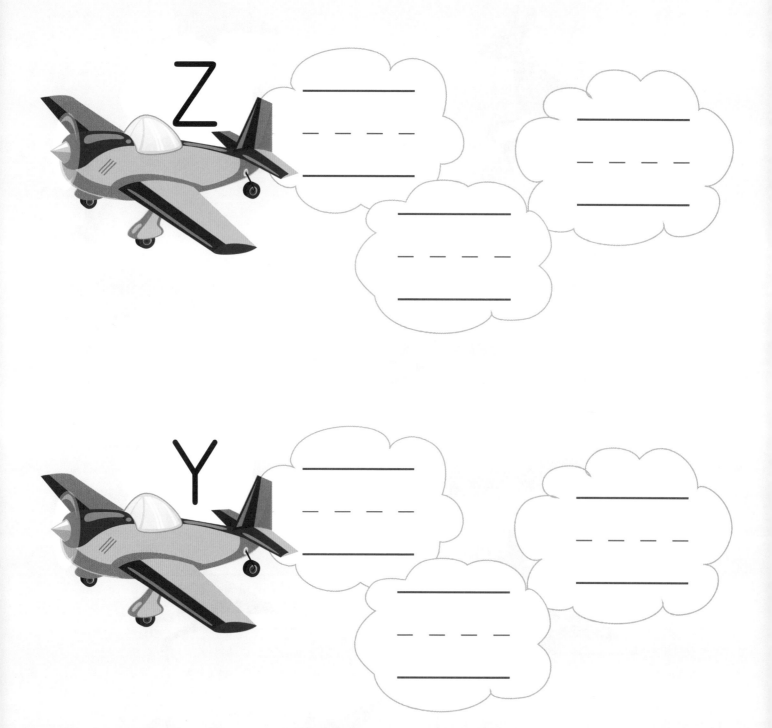

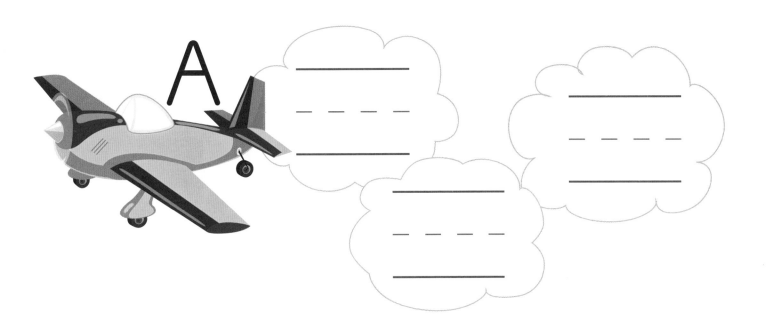

Uppercase D

Write the Letter D

TRACE the uppercase letter D. Start at the green arrow labeled with a number 1.

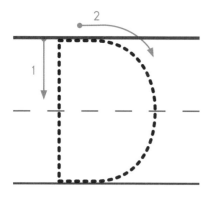

Dog

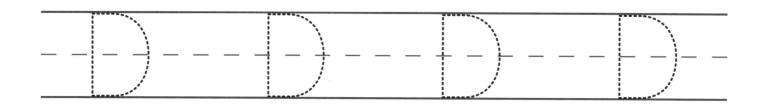

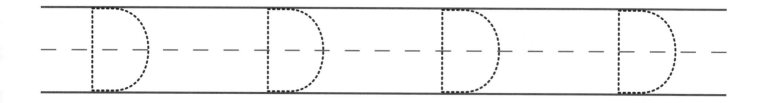

Now WRITE four uppercase D's.

1   2   3   4

68

Letter Blocks

WRITE **D** in the empty blocks.

Uppercase D

Name Game

WRITE **D** in each space to see each child's name.

HELLO **David**

HELLO ___aisy

HELLO ___an

HELLO ___elia

HELLO ___ottie

HELLO ___erek

D Is for Drum

WRITE **D** on each drum.

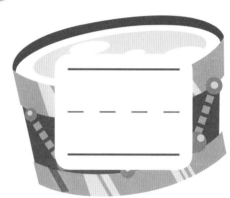

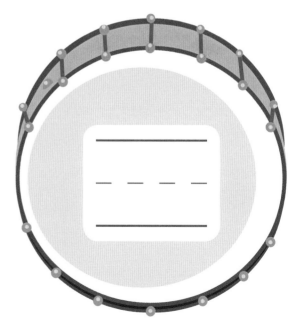

Uppercase P

Write the Letter P

TRACE the uppercase letter **P**. Start at the green arrow labeled with a number 1.

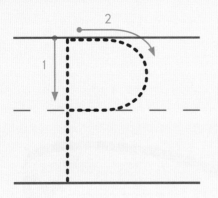

Pig

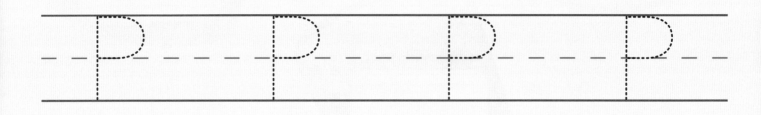

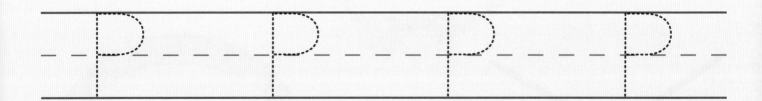

Now WRITE four uppercase **P**'s.

1   2   3   4

Letter Blocks

WRITE **P** in the empty blocks.

Deliver the Letter

WRITE **P** in each space to finish addressing the letter.

Patty _igeon

789 _each __l.

__eckville, __A

18452

Grocery List

WRITE **P** in each space to finish the grocery list.

P ie

___ ineapple

___ izza

___ ear

___ opcorn

Write the Letter R

TRACE the uppercase letter **R**. Start at the green arrow labeled with a number 1.

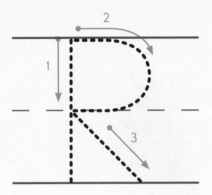

Rose

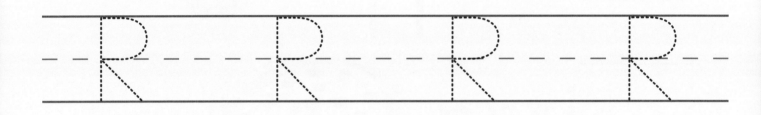

Now WRITE four uppercase **R**'s.

1   2   3   4

Letter Blocks

WRITE **R** in the empty blocks.

Stitch It Up

WRITE **R** in each square to finish the quilt.

R Is for Robot

WRITE **R** on each robot.

Write the Letter B

TRACE the uppercase letter **B**. Start at the green arrow labeled with a number 1.

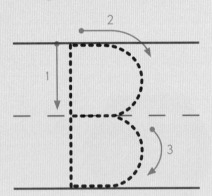

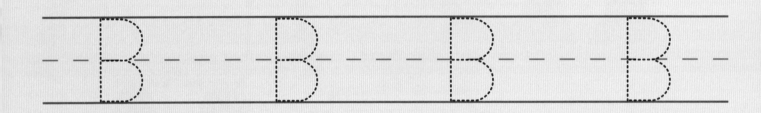

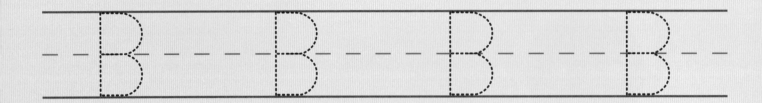

Now WRITE four uppercase **B**'s.

1   2   3   4

Letter Blocks

WRITE **B** in the empty blocks.

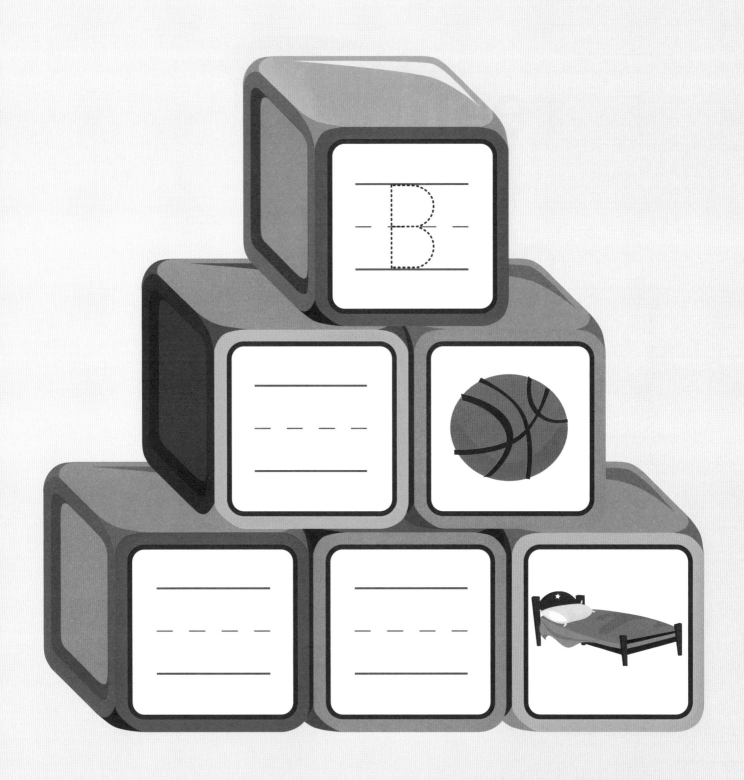

Uppercase B

Grocery List

WRITE **B** in each space to finish the grocery list.

B read

____ anana

____ roccoli

____ utter

____ lueberries

B Is for Ball

WRITE **B** on each ball.

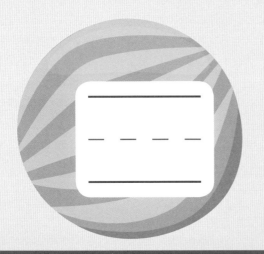

Uppercase U

Write the Letter U

TRACE the uppercase letter **U**. Start at the green arrow labeled with a number 1.

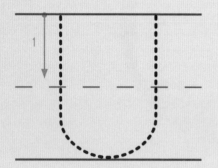

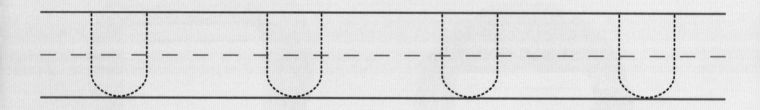

Now WRITE four uppercase **U**'s.

1   2   3   4

Letter Blocks

WRITE **U** in the empty blocks.

Uppercase U

Stitch It Up

WRITE **U** in each square to finish the quilt.

U Is for Umbrella

WRITE **U** on each umbrella.

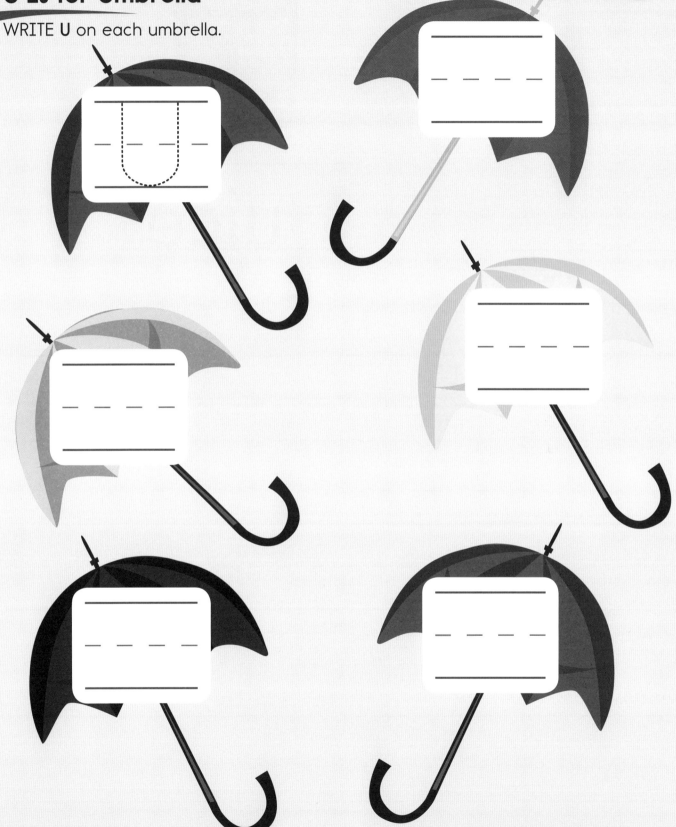

Write the Letter J

TRACE the uppercase letter **J**. Start at the green arrow labeled with a number 1.

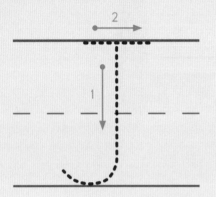

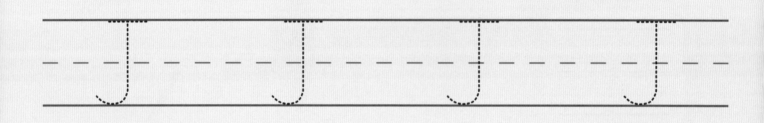

Now WRITE four uppercase **J**'s.

1   2   3   4

Letter Blocks

WRITE **J** in the empty blocks.

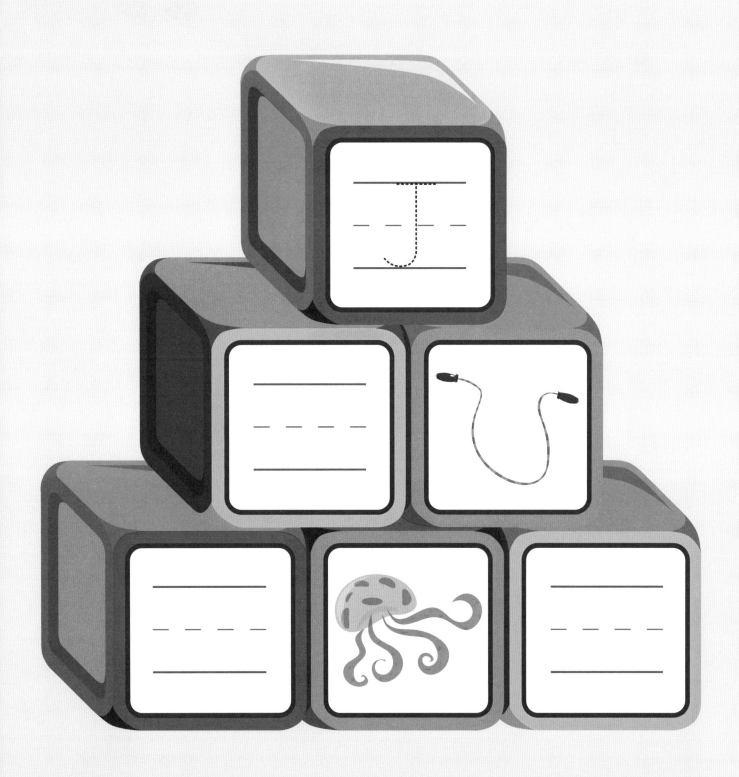

Uppercase J

Letter Connection

WRITE **J** in each space to connect the jellybeans.

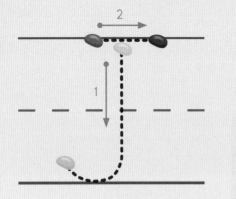

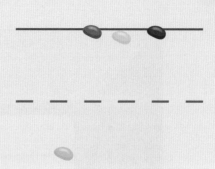

Tongue Twisting Time

WRITE **J** in each space to
complete the tongue twister.

Jolly ___asper

___ellyfish

___uggles ___ugs

of ___uice

Triple Play

TRACE each letter. Then WRITE it three times.

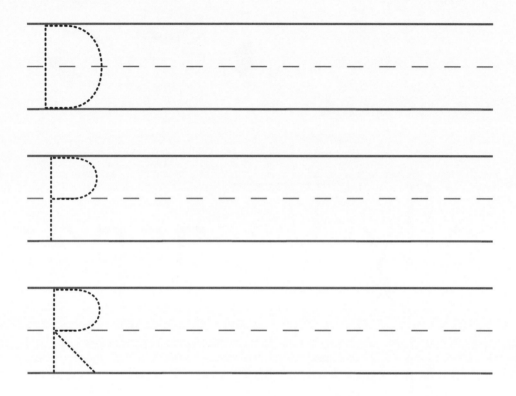

WRITE **D**, **P**, and **R** in the blocks.

Triple Play

TRACE each letter. Then WRITE it three times.

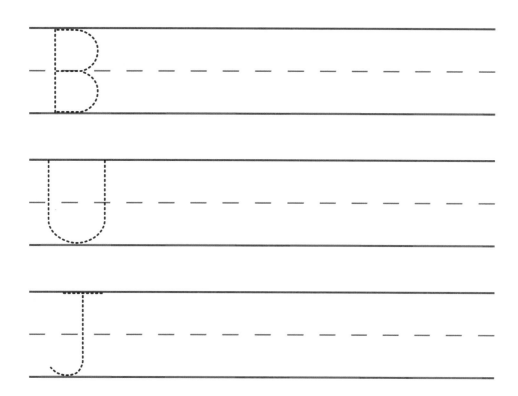

WRITE **B**, **U**, and **J** in the blocks.

Uppercase C

Write the Letter C

TRACE the uppercase letter **C**. Start at the green arrow labeled with a number 1.

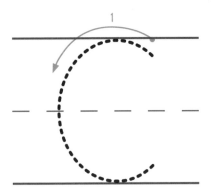

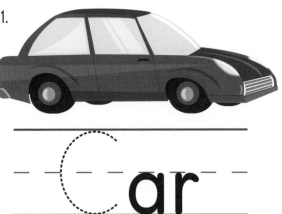

Car

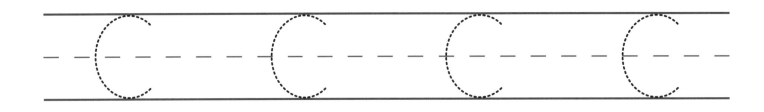

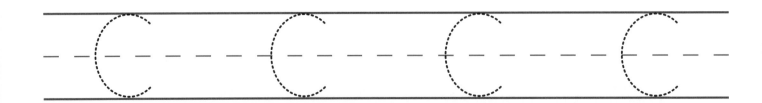

Now WRITE four uppercase **C**'s.

1   2   3   4

Letter Blocks

WRITE C in the empty blocks.

Deliver the Letter

WRITE **C** in each space to finish addressing the letter.

33¢

C ate C aterpillar

321 C ocoon St.

C rescent, C A

95531

Letter Connection

WRITE **C** in each space to connect the cookies.

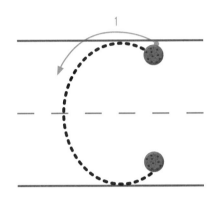

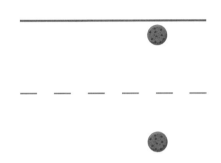

Uppercase G

Write the Letter G

TRACE the uppercase letter **G**. Start at the green arrow labeled with a number 1.

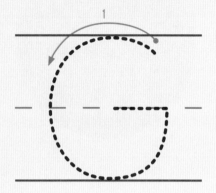

Goat

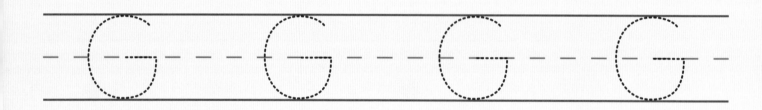

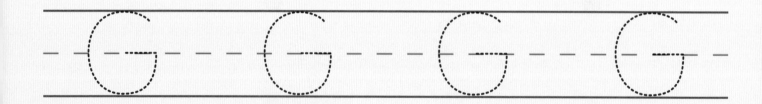

Now WRITE four uppercase **G**'s.

1   2   3   4

98

Letter Blocks

WRITE **G** in the empty blocks.

Uppercase G

Name Game

WRITE **G** in each space to see each child's name.

HELLO
George

HELLO
___inny

HELLO
___erry

HELLO
___ail

HELLO
___ina

HELLO
___rant

Tongue Twisting Time

WRITE **G** in each space to
complete the tongue twister.

Gilda __oldfish

__rinned in

__olden __litter

__lasses

Uppercase O

Write the Letter O

TRACE the uppercase letter **O**. Start at the green arrow labeled with a number 1.

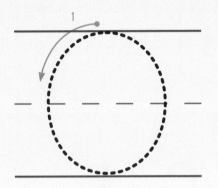

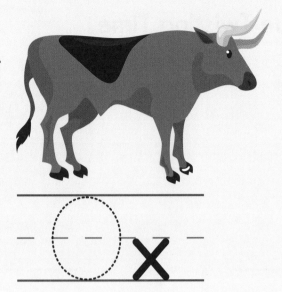

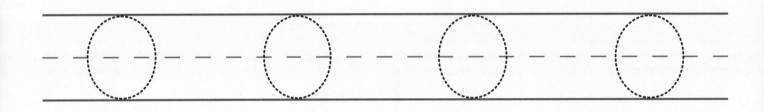

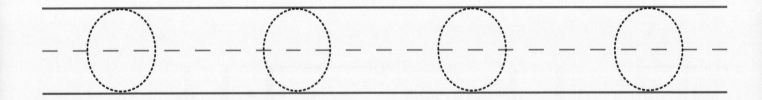

Now WRITE four uppercase **O**'s.

1   2   3   4

Letter Blocks

WRITE O in the empty blocks.

Uppercase O

Write It Right

WRITE **O** on each canister of oatmeal.

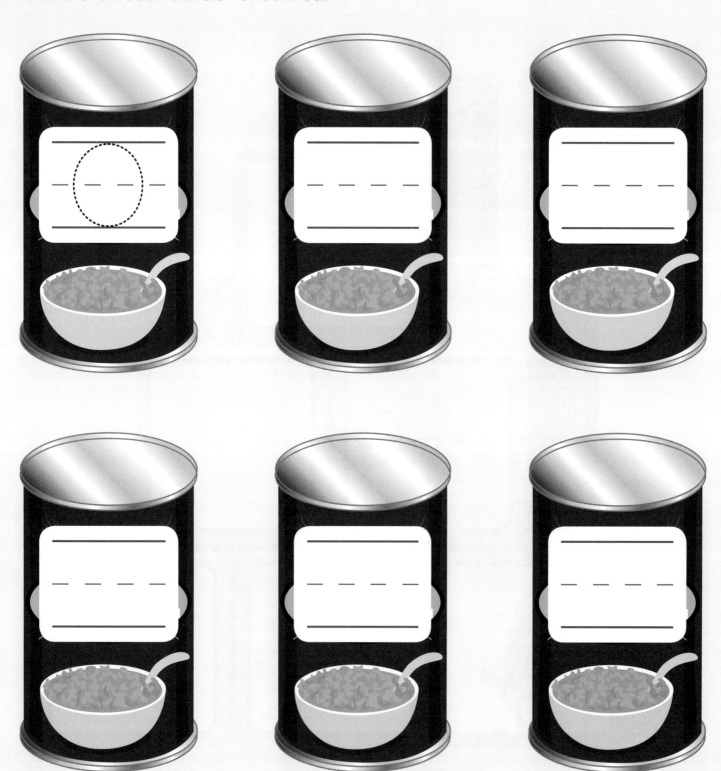

Grocery List

WRITE O in each space to finish the grocery list.

___O nion

_____ live

_____ atmeal

_____ il

_____ range

Uppercase Q

Write the Letter Q

TRACE the uppercase letter **Q**. Start at the green arrow labeled with a number 1.

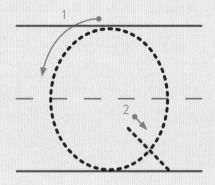

Queen

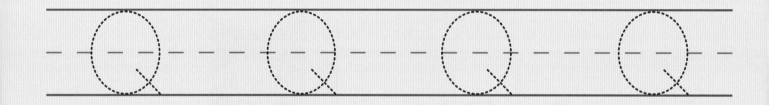

Now WRITE four uppercase **Q**'s.

_____

- - - - - - - - - - - - - - - - - - - -

_____

| 1 | 2 | 3 | 4 |

Letter Blocks

WRITE Q in the empty blocks.

Uppercase Q

Stitch It Up

WRITE **Q** in each square to finish the quilt.

Q Is for Quail

WRITE **Q** on each quail.

Uppercase S

Write the Letter S

TRACE the uppercase letter **S**. Start at the green arrow labeled with a number 1.

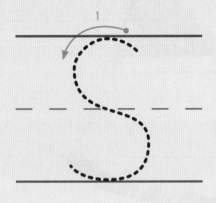

S oup

S   S   S   S

S   S   S   S

Now WRITE four uppercase **S**'s.

1   2   3   4

Letter Blocks

WRITE **S** in the empty blocks.

Deliver the Letter

WRITE S in each space to finish addressing the letter.

S tacy ___tarfish

910 ___ and ___t.

___ eabrook, ___C

29940

S Is for Sun

WRITE **S** on each sun.

Review

Skywriting

WRITE the letters in the clouds following each airplane.

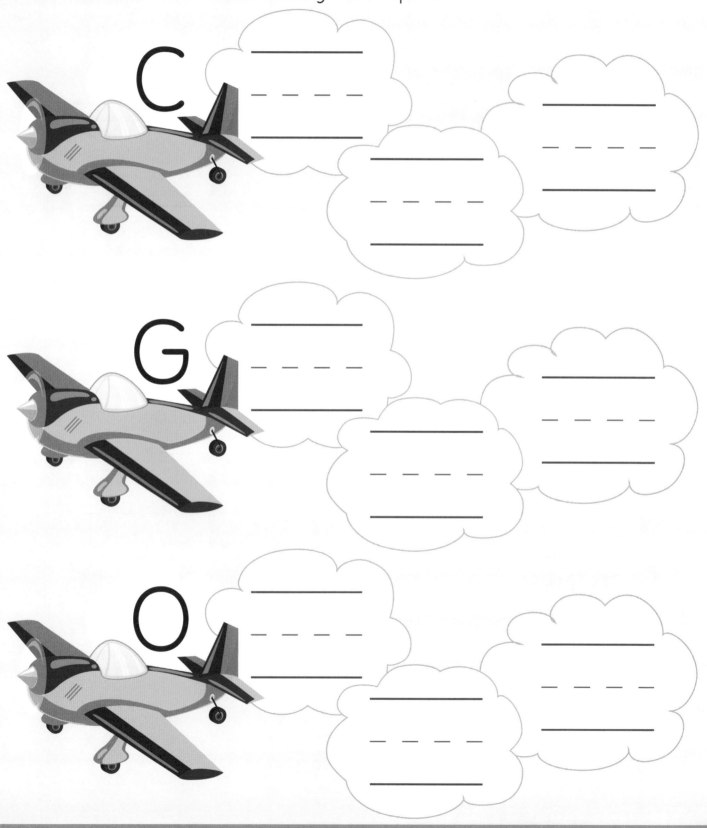

Sign Sightings

WRITE the words inside the signs.

GAS

BUS

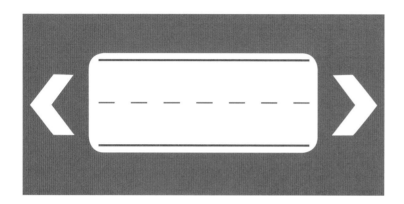

EXIT

TAXI

Sign Sightings

WRITE the words inside the signs.

STOP

FOOD

WALK

SALE

All Together Now

TRACE the uppercase letters of the alphabet in order.

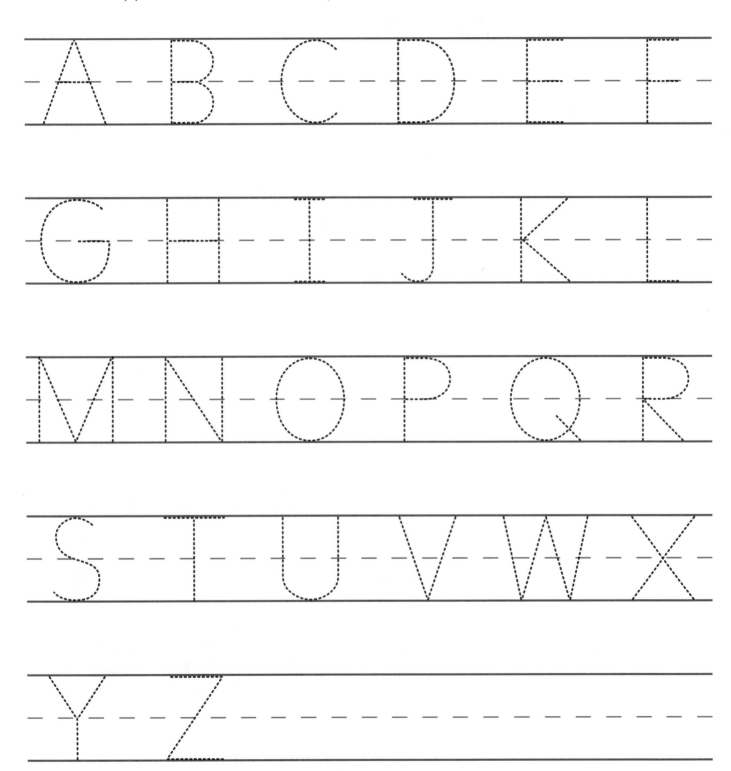

On Your Own

WRITE the uppercase letters of the alphabet in order.

Letters Everywhere

Alphabet Soup

WRITE any uppercase letters you choose in the bowl of alphabet soup!

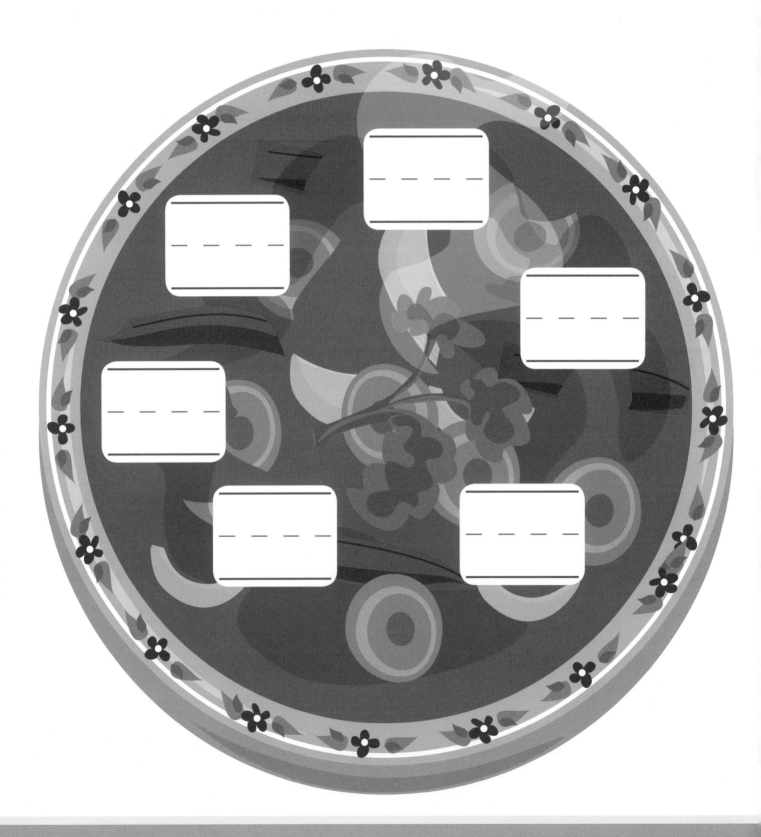